T0193557

A Night at the Park with
Jesus

Written by **Laura Silva**
Illustrated by **Alana Wilson**

WestBow Press books may be ordered through booksellers or by contacting:

WestBow Press
A Division of Thomas Nelson & Zondervan
1663 Liberty Drive
Bloomington, IN 47403
www.westbowpress.com
844-714-3454

Because of the dynamic nature of the Internet, any web addresses or links contained in this book may have changed since publication and may no longer be valid. The views expressed in this work are solely those of the author and do not necessarily reflect the views of the publisher, and the publisher hereby disclaims any responsibility for them.

Interior Image Credit: Alana Wilson

Scripture quotations marked NLT are taken from the Holy Bible, New Living Translation, Copyright © 1996, 2004, 2015 by Tyndale House Foundation. Used by permission of Tyndale House Publishers, Inc., Carol Stream, Illinois 60188. All rights reserved.

Scripture quotations marked NKJV are taken from the New King James Version®. Copyright © 1982 by Thomas Nelson. Used by permission. All rights reserved.

ISBN: 978-1-6642-9924-5 (sc)
978-1-6642-9923-8 (e)

Library of Congress Control Number: 2023908496

Print information available on the last page.

WestBow Press rev. date: 07/07/2023

WESTBOW
PRESS®
A DIVISION OF THOMAS NELSON
& ZONDERVAN

God will never leave you nor forsake you.

— Hebrews 13:5 (NKJV)

The playground was Sofia's favourite

place in the whole wide world.

Every day, she spent long hours

playing and having fun at the park.

Sofia loved going up and down on the teeter-totter.

She also liked to soar high on the swing,

so high she could almost touch the clouds!

Sofia's all-time favourite was spinning super-fast
on the roundabout until she felt dizzy.

After long days at the park, right before bed,
Sofia liked to gather all her stuffed animals around her
and sing songs to her friend Jesus.

She would then snuggle into bed and fall asleep,
having sweet dreams until the morning.

One night, Sofia dreamed that a brilliant light shone
through her window, illuminating the whole room.
She got up and saw the figure of a man
as bright as the sun.

Sofia then heard a warm and sweet
voice greet her from the
radiant glow of light.
It was her friend Jesus!

Sofia rubbed her eyes, and the light slowly dimmed
as He came further into the room. When she opened her
eyes, Sofia could see that her dear friend Jesus had
indeed come to visit. She smiled from ear to ear.

She was very excited to see Him. She jumped out of
bed and gave Him an enormous hug!

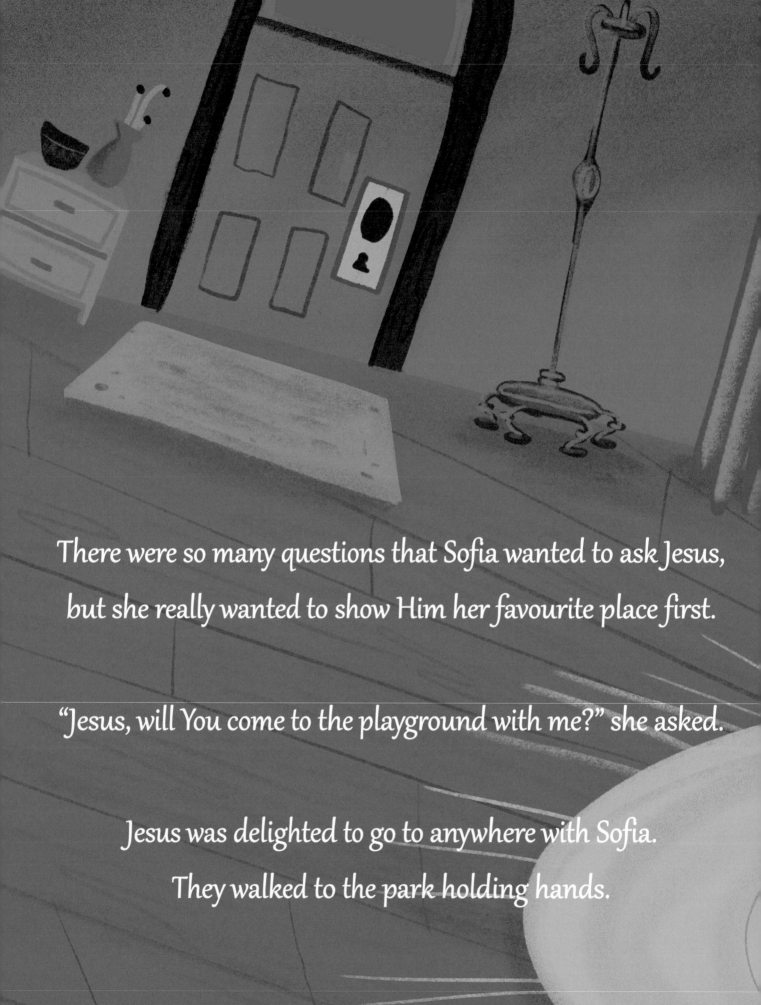

There were so many questions that Sofia wanted to ask Jesus,
but she really wanted to show Him her favourite place first.

"Jesus, will You come to the playground with me?" she asked.

Jesus was delighted to go to anywhere with Sofia.
They walked to the park holding hands.

When they got to the park, Sofia was surprised to find that the night had turned into day. She looked up at Jesus and noticed that He was smiling.

"Do You like the playground, Jesus?" Sofia asked.

Jesus smiled.

He loved being with Sofia at the park.

"Amazing! I'll race You to the slides then!" Sofia exclaimed.

Jesus and Sofia ran as fast as they could
and then hurtled down the slides together.

"Whoo-hoo!" they shouted joyfully.
Next, they spun on the roundabout.

"Could You please make it go faster?" Sofia asked.

So, Jesus whirled the roundabout
faster and faster, around and around.

Sofia was enjoying the playground more than ever before.

WHEEE!

Next, they went up and down on the teeter-totter.

Then, they jumped onto the swings and soared
so high they almost touched the clouds!
Jesus and Sofia laughed with glee.

When they arrived home, Jesus took her into His arms and thanked her for an incredible time together and for showing Him her favourite place. He reminded her to never forget that He was her friend, that He loved her, and that He was always with her. Jesus made sure Sofia knew that whenever she felt sad or afraid, He would comfort her with His love, strengthen her with His power, and give her His peace at all times. Jesus told Sofia that she could talk to Him at any time of the day; He was just a prayer away.

Sofia's heart filled with joy because she knew

that Jesus loved her and cared for her.

When Sofia woke up in the morning, she looked

out the window at the park and felt like the

happiest girl alive. What a wonderful dream,

she thought. *Thank You, dear Jesus, for visiting*

me in my dream last night. Thank You for your

friendship and love. I will invite You everywhere I

go from now on, because being with You is

awesome. Amen.

"I no longer call you servants, because a servant does not know his master's business. Instead, I have called you friends, for everything that I learned from my Father I have made known to you."

- John 15:15 (NLT)

Printed in the United States
by Baker & Taylor Publisher Services